THE LIBRARY OF

_____

DIGITAL BOOK JOURNALING!
BOOKJOURNAL.APP
TRY CREATING A DIGITAL COPY OF YOUR #BOOKTOK JOURNAL FOR FREE! AVAILABLE ON ANY BROWSER!

BOOK COVER
4.25IN X 2.75IN

TITLE:
AUTHOR:
GENRE:
METHOD:
DATE STARTED:
DATE FINISHED:
WOULD YOU RECOMMEND?
NOTES & QUOTES:

★★★★★

BOOK COVER
4.25IN X 2.75IN

TITLE:
AUTHOR:
GENRE:
METHOD:
DATE STARTED:
DATE FINISHED:
WOULD YOU RECOMMEND?
NOTES & QUOTES:

★★★★★

BOOK COVER
4.25IN X 2.75IN

TITLE:

AUTHOR:

GENRE:

METHOD:

DATE STARTED:

DATE FINISHED:

WOULD YOU RECOMMEND?

NOTES & QUOTES:

BOOK COVER
4.25IN X 2.75IN

TITLE:

AUTHOR:

GENRE:

METHOD:

DATE STARTED:

DATE FINISHED:

WOULD YOU RECOMMEND?

NOTES & QUOTES:

BOOK COVER
4.25IN X 2.75IN

TITLE:

AUTHOR:

GENRE:

METHOD:

DATE STARTED:

DATE FINISHED:

WOULD YOU RECOMMEND?

NOTES & QUOTES:

BOOK COVER
4.25IN X 2.75IN

TITLE:

AUTHOR:

GENRE:

METHOD:

DATE STARTED:

DATE FINISHED:

WOULD YOU RECOMMEND?

NOTES & QUOTES:

BOOK COVER
4.25IN X 2.75IN

TITLE:

AUTHOR:

GENRE:

METHOD:

DATE STARTED:

DATE FINISHED:

WOULD YOU RECOMMEND?

NOTES & QUOTES:

BOOK COVER
4.25IN X 2.75IN

TITLE:

AUTHOR:

GENRE:

METHOD:

DATE STARTED:

DATE FINISHED:

WOULD YOU RECOMMEND?

NOTES & QUOTES:

BOOK COVER
4.25IN X 2.75IN

TITLE:
AUTHOR:
GENRE:
METHOD:
DATE STARTED:
DATE FINISHED:
WOULD YOU RECOMMEND?
NOTES & QUOTES:

⭐⭐⭐⭐⭐

BOOK COVER
4.25IN X 2.75IN

TITLE:
AUTHOR:
GENRE:
METHOD:
DATE STARTED:
DATE FINISHED:
WOULD YOU RECOMMEND?
NOTES & QUOTES:

⭐⭐⭐⭐⭐

BOOK COVER
4.25IN X 2.75IN

TITLE:
AUTHOR:
GENRE:
METHOD:
DATE STARTED:
DATE FINISHED:
WOULD YOU RECOMMEND?
NOTES & QUOTES:

★★★★★

BOOK COVER
4.25IN X 2.75IN

TITLE:
AUTHOR:
GENRE:
METHOD:
DATE STARTED:
DATE FINISHED:
WOULD YOU RECOMMEND?
NOTES & QUOTES:

★★★★★

BOOK COVER
4.25IN X 2.75IN

TITLE: _____
AUTHOR: _____
GENRE: _____
METHOD: _____
DATE STARTED: _____
DATE FINISHED: _____
WOULD YOU RECOMMEND? _____
NOTES & QUOTES:

BOOK COVER
4.25IN X 2.75IN

TITLE: _____
AUTHOR: _____
GENRE: _____
METHOD: _____
DATE STARTED: _____
DATE FINISHED: _____
WOULD YOU RECOMMEND? _____
NOTES & QUOTES:

BOOK COVER 4.25IN X 2.75IN	TITLE: _____ AUTHOR: _____ GENRE: _____ METHOD: _____ DATE STARTED: _____ DATE FINISHED: _____ WOULD YOU RECOMMEND? _____ NOTES & QUOTES:
☆☆☆☆☆	
BOOK COVER 4.25IN X 2.75IN	TITLE: _____ AUTHOR: _____ GENRE: _____ METHOD: _____ DATE STARTED: _____ DATE FINISHED: _____ WOULD YOU RECOMMEND? _____ NOTES & QUOTES:
☆☆☆☆☆	

BOOK COVER
4.25IN X 2.75IN

TITLE:

AUTHOR:

GENRE:

METHOD:

DATE STARTED:

DATE FINISHED:

WOULD YOU RECOMMEND?

NOTES & QUOTES:

BOOK COVER
4.25IN X 2.75IN

TITLE:

AUTHOR:

GENRE:

METHOD:

DATE STARTED:

DATE FINISHED:

WOULD YOU RECOMMEND?

NOTES & QUOTES:

BOOK COVER
4.25IN X 2.75IN

TITLE:
AUTHOR:
GENRE:
METHOD:
DATE STARTED:
DATE FINISHED:
WOULD YOU RECOMMEND?
NOTES & QUOTES:

⭐⭐⭐⭐⭐

BOOK COVER
4.25IN X 2.75IN

TITLE:
AUTHOR:
GENRE:
METHOD:
DATE STARTED:
DATE FINISHED:
WOULD YOU RECOMMEND?
NOTES & QUOTES:

⭐⭐⭐⭐⭐

BOOK COVER
4.25IN X 2.75IN

TITLE:

AUTHOR:

GENRE:

METHOD:

DATE STARTED:

DATE FINISHED:

WOULD YOU RECOMMEND?

NOTES & QUOTES:

BOOK COVER
4.25IN X 2.75IN

TITLE:

AUTHOR:

GENRE:

METHOD:

DATE STARTED:

DATE FINISHED:

WOULD YOU RECOMMEND?

NOTES & QUOTES:

BOOK COVER
4.25IN X 2.75IN

TITLE:

AUTHOR:

GENRE:

METHOD:

DATE STARTED:

DATE FINISHED:

WOULD YOU RECOMMEND?

NOTES & QUOTES:

☆☆☆☆☆

BOOK COVER
4.25IN X 2.75IN

TITLE:

AUTHOR:

GENRE:

METHOD:

DATE STARTED:

DATE FINISHED:

WOULD YOU RECOMMEND?

NOTES & QUOTES:

☆☆☆☆☆

BOOK COVER
4.25IN X 2.75IN

TITLE:

AUTHOR:

GENRE:

METHOD:

DATE STARTED:

DATE FINISHED:

WOULD YOU RECOMMEND?

NOTES & QUOTES:

★★★★★

BOOK COVER
4.25IN X 2.75IN

TITLE:

AUTHOR:

GENRE:

METHOD:

DATE STARTED:

DATE FINISHED:

WOULD YOU RECOMMEND?

NOTES & QUOTES:

★★★★★

BOOK COVER
4.25IN X 2.75IN

TITLE: _____
AUTHOR: _____
GENRE: _____
METHOD: _____
DATE STARTED: _____
DATE FINISHED: _____
WOULD YOU RECOMMEND? _____
NOTES & QUOTES:

⭐⭐⭐⭐⭐

BOOK COVER
4.25IN X 2.75IN

TITLE: _____
AUTHOR: _____
GENRE: _____
METHOD: _____
DATE STARTED: _____
DATE FINISHED: _____
WOULD YOU RECOMMEND? _____
NOTES & QUOTES:

⭐⭐⭐⭐⭐

BOOK COVER
4.25IN X 2.75IN

TITLE:

AUTHOR:

GENRE:

METHOD:

DATE STARTED:

DATE FINISHED:

WOULD YOU RECOMMEND?

NOTES & QUOTES:

★★★★★

BOOK COVER
4.25IN X 2.75IN

TITLE:

AUTHOR:

GENRE:

METHOD:

DATE STARTED:

DATE FINISHED:

WOULD YOU RECOMMEND?

NOTES & QUOTES:

★★★★★

BOOK COVER
4.25IN X 2.75IN

TITLE: _____
AUTHOR: _____
GENRE: _____
METHOD: _____
DATE STARTED: _____
DATE FINISHED: _____
WOULD YOU RECOMMEND? _____
NOTES & QUOTES:

☆ ☆ ☆ ☆ ☆

BOOK COVER
4.25IN X 2.75IN

TITLE: _____
AUTHOR: _____
GENRE: _____
METHOD: _____
DATE STARTED: _____
DATE FINISHED: _____
WOULD YOU RECOMMEND? _____
NOTES & QUOTES:

☆ ☆ ☆ ☆ ☆

BOOK COVER
4.25IN X 2.75IN

TITLE:
AUTHOR:
GENRE:
METHOD:
DATE STARTED:
DATE FINISHED:
WOULD YOU RECOMMEND?
NOTES & QUOTES:

★★★★★

BOOK COVER
4.25IN X 2.75IN

TITLE:
AUTHOR:
GENRE:
METHOD:
DATE STARTED:
DATE FINISHED:
WOULD YOU RECOMMEND?
NOTES & QUOTES:

★★★★★

BOOK COVER
4.25IN X 2.75IN

TITLE:

AUTHOR:

GENRE:

METHOD:

DATE STARTED:

DATE FINISHED:

WOULD YOU RECOMMEND?

NOTES & QUOTES:

BOOK COVER
4.25IN X 2.75IN

TITLE:

AUTHOR:

GENRE:

METHOD:

DATE STARTED:

DATE FINISHED:

WOULD YOU RECOMMEND?

NOTES & QUOTES:

BOOK COVER
4.25IN X 2.75IN

TITLE:

AUTHOR:

GENRE:

METHOD:

DATE STARTED:

DATE FINISHED:

WOULD YOU RECOMMEND?

NOTES & QUOTES:

BOOK COVER
4.25IN X 2.75IN

TITLE:

AUTHOR:

GENRE:

METHOD:

DATE STARTED:

DATE FINISHED:

WOULD YOU RECOMMEND?

NOTES & QUOTES:

BOOK COVER
4.25IN X 2.75IN

TITLE: _____
AUTHOR: _____
GENRE: _____
METHOD: _____
DATE STARTED: _____
DATE FINISHED: _____
WOULD YOU RECOMMEND? _____
NOTES & QUOTES:

☆ ☆ ☆ ☆ ☆

BOOK COVER
4.25IN X 2.75IN

TITLE: _____
AUTHOR: _____
GENRE: _____
METHOD: _____
DATE STARTED: _____
DATE FINISHED: _____
WOULD YOU RECOMMEND? _____
NOTES & QUOTES:

☆ ☆ ☆ ☆ ☆

BOOK COVER
4.25IN X 2.75IN

TITLE:
AUTHOR:
GENRE:
METHOD:
DATE STARTED:
DATE FINISHED:
WOULD YOU RECOMMEND?
NOTES & QUOTES:

★★★★★

BOOK COVER
4.25IN X 2.75IN

TITLE:
AUTHOR:
GENRE:
METHOD:
DATE STARTED:
DATE FINISHED:
WOULD YOU RECOMMEND?
NOTES & QUOTES:

★★★★★

BOOK COVER
4.25IN X 2.75IN

TITLE:

AUTHOR:

GENRE:

METHOD:

DATE STARTED:

DATE FINISHED:

WOULD YOU RECOMMEND?

NOTES & QUOTES:

BOOK COVER
4.25IN X 2.75IN

TITLE:

AUTHOR:

GENRE:

METHOD:

DATE STARTED:

DATE FINISHED:

WOULD YOU RECOMMEND?

NOTES & QUOTES:

BOOK COVER
4.25IN X 2.75IN

TITLE: _____
AUTHOR: _____
GENRE: _____
METHOD: _____
DATE STARTED: _____
DATE FINISHED: _____
WOULD YOU RECOMMEND? _____
NOTES & QUOTES:

★★★★★

BOOK COVER
4.25IN X 2.75IN

TITLE: _____
AUTHOR: _____
GENRE: _____
METHOD: _____
DATE STARTED: _____
DATE FINISHED: _____
WOULD YOU RECOMMEND? _____
NOTES & QUOTES:

★★★★★

BOOK COVER
4.25IN X 2.75IN

TITLE:

AUTHOR:

GENRE:

METHOD:

DATE STARTED:

DATE FINISHED:

WOULD YOU RECOMMEND?

NOTES & QUOTES:

BOOK COVER
4.25IN X 2.75IN

TITLE:

AUTHOR:

GENRE:

METHOD:

DATE STARTED:

DATE FINISHED:

WOULD YOU RECOMMEND?

NOTES & QUOTES:

BOOK COVER
4.25IN X 2.75IN

TITLE:
AUTHOR:
GENRE:
METHOD:
DATE STARTED:
DATE FINISHED:
WOULD YOU RECOMMEND?
NOTES & QUOTES:

BOOK COVER
4.25IN X 2.75IN

TITLE:
AUTHOR:
GENRE:
METHOD:
DATE STARTED:
DATE FINISHED:
WOULD YOU RECOMMEND?
NOTES & QUOTES:

BOOK COVER
4.25IN X 2.75IN

TITLE:

AUTHOR:

GENRE:

METHOD:

DATE STARTED:

DATE FINISHED:

WOULD YOU RECOMMEND?

NOTES & QUOTES:

BOOK COVER
4.25IN X 2.75IN

TITLE:

AUTHOR:

GENRE:

METHOD:

DATE STARTED:

DATE FINISHED:

WOULD YOU RECOMMEND?

NOTES & QUOTES:

BOOK COVER
4.25IN X 2.75IN

TITLE:
AUTHOR:
GENRE:
METHOD:
DATE STARTED:
DATE FINISHED:
WOULD YOU RECOMMEND?
NOTES & QUOTES:

BOOK COVER
4.25IN X 2.75IN

TITLE:
AUTHOR:
GENRE:
METHOD:
DATE STARTED:
DATE FINISHED:
WOULD YOU RECOMMEND?
NOTES & QUOTES:

BOOK COVER
4.25IN X 2.75IN

TITLE:
AUTHOR:
GENRE:
METHOD:
DATE STARTED:
DATE FINISHED:
WOULD YOU RECOMMEND?
NOTES & QUOTES:

★ ★ ★ ★ ★

BOOK COVER
4.25IN X 2.75IN

TITLE:
AUTHOR:
GENRE:
METHOD:
DATE STARTED:
DATE FINISHED:
WOULD YOU RECOMMEND?
NOTES & QUOTES:

★ ★ ★ ★ ★

BOOK COVER
4.25IN X 2.75IN

TITLE: _____
AUTHOR: _____
GENRE: _____
METHOD: _____
DATE STARTED: _____
DATE FINISHED: _____
WOULD YOU RECOMMEND? _____
NOTES & QUOTES:

★★★★★

BOOK COVER
4.25IN X 2.75IN

TITLE: _____
AUTHOR: _____
GENRE: _____
METHOD: _____
DATE STARTED: _____
DATE FINISHED: _____
WOULD YOU RECOMMEND? _____
NOTES & QUOTES:

★★★★★

BOOK COVER
4.25IN X 2.75IN

TITLE:
AUTHOR:
GENRE:
METHOD:
DATE STARTED:
DATE FINISHED:
WOULD YOU RECOMMEND?
NOTES & QUOTES:

BOOK COVER
4.25IN X 2.75IN

TITLE:
AUTHOR:
GENRE:
METHOD:
DATE STARTED:
DATE FINISHED:
WOULD YOU RECOMMEND?
NOTES & QUOTES:

BOOK COVER
4.25IN X 2.75IN

TITLE:
AUTHOR:
GENRE:
METHOD:
DATE STARTED:
DATE FINISHED:
WOULD YOU RECOMMEND?
NOTES & QUOTES:

BOOK COVER
4.25IN X 2.75IN

TITLE:
AUTHOR:
GENRE:
METHOD:
DATE STARTED:
DATE FINISHED:
WOULD YOU RECOMMEND?
NOTES & QUOTES:

BOOK COVER
4.25IN X 2.75IN

TITLE:
AUTHOR:
GENRE:
METHOD:
DATE STARTED:
DATE FINISHED:
WOULD YOU RECOMMEND?
NOTES & QUOTES:

BOOK COVER
4.25IN X 2.75IN

TITLE:
AUTHOR:
GENRE:
METHOD:
DATE STARTED:
DATE FINISHED:
WOULD YOU RECOMMEND?
NOTES & QUOTES:

BOOK COVER
4.25IN X 2.75IN

TITLE:

AUTHOR:

GENRE:

METHOD:

DATE STARTED:

DATE FINISHED:

WOULD YOU RECOMMEND?

NOTES & QUOTES:

BOOK COVER
4.25IN X 2.75IN

TITLE:

AUTHOR:

GENRE:

METHOD:

DATE STARTED:

DATE FINISHED:

WOULD YOU RECOMMEND?

NOTES & QUOTES:

BOOK COVER
4.25IN X 2.75IN

TITLE:
AUTHOR:
GENRE:
METHOD:
DATE STARTED:
DATE FINISHED:
WOULD YOU RECOMMEND?
NOTES & QUOTES:

BOOK COVER
4.25IN X 2.75IN

TITLE:
AUTHOR:
GENRE:
METHOD:
DATE STARTED:
DATE FINISHED:
WOULD YOU RECOMMEND?
NOTES & QUOTES:

BOOK COVER
4.25IN X 2.75IN

TITLE:

AUTHOR:

GENRE:

METHOD:

DATE STARTED:

DATE FINISHED:

WOULD YOU RECOMMEND?

NOTES & QUOTES:

BOOK COVER
4.25IN X 2.75IN

TITLE:

AUTHOR:

GENRE:

METHOD:

DATE STARTED:

DATE FINISHED:

WOULD YOU RECOMMEND?

NOTES & QUOTES:

BOOK COVER
4.25IN X 2.75IN

TITLE: _____
AUTHOR: _____
GENRE: _____
METHOD: _____
DATE STARTED: _____
DATE FINISHED: _____
WOULD YOU RECOMMEND? _____
NOTES & QUOTES:

BOOK COVER
4.25IN X 2.75IN

TITLE: _____
AUTHOR: _____
GENRE: _____
METHOD: _____
DATE STARTED: _____
DATE FINISHED: _____
WOULD YOU RECOMMEND? _____
NOTES & QUOTES:

BOOK COVER
4.25IN X 2.75IN

TITLE:
AUTHOR:
GENRE:
METHOD:
DATE STARTED:
DATE FINISHED:
WOULD YOU RECOMMEND?
NOTES & QUOTES:

BOOK COVER
4.25IN X 2.75IN

TITLE:
AUTHOR:
GENRE:
METHOD:
DATE STARTED:
DATE FINISHED:
WOULD YOU RECOMMEND?
NOTES & QUOTES:

BOOK COVER
4.25IN X 2.75IN

TITLE:

AUTHOR:

GENRE:

METHOD:

DATE STARTED:

DATE FINISHED:

WOULD YOU RECOMMEND?

NOTES & QUOTES:

⭐⭐⭐⭐⭐

BOOK COVER
4.25IN X 2.75IN

TITLE:

AUTHOR:

GENRE:

METHOD:

DATE STARTED:

DATE FINISHED:

WOULD YOU RECOMMEND?

NOTES & QUOTES:

⭐⭐⭐⭐⭐

BOOK COVER
4.25IN X 2.75IN

TITLE:

AUTHOR:

GENRE:

METHOD:

DATE STARTED:

DATE FINISHED:

WOULD YOU RECOMMEND?

NOTES & QUOTES:

★★★★★

BOOK COVER
4.25IN X 2.75IN

TITLE:

AUTHOR:

GENRE:

METHOD:

DATE STARTED:

DATE FINISHED:

WOULD YOU RECOMMEND?

NOTES & QUOTES:

★★★★★

BOOK COVER
4.25IN X 2.75IN

TITLE:
AUTHOR:
GENRE:
METHOD:
DATE STARTED:
DATE FINISHED:
WOULD YOU RECOMMEND?
NOTES & QUOTES:

★ ★ ★ ★ ★

BOOK COVER
4.25IN X 2.75IN

TITLE:
AUTHOR:
GENRE:
METHOD:
DATE STARTED:
DATE FINISHED:
WOULD YOU RECOMMEND?
NOTES & QUOTES:

★ ★ ★ ★ ★

BOOK COVER
4.25IN X 2.75IN

TITLE:
AUTHOR:
GENRE:
METHOD:
DATE STARTED:
DATE FINISHED:
WOULD YOU RECOMMEND?
NOTES & QUOTES:

BOOK COVER
4.25IN X 2.75IN

TITLE:
AUTHOR:
GENRE:
METHOD:
DATE STARTED:
DATE FINISHED:
WOULD YOU RECOMMEND?
NOTES & QUOTES:

BOOK COVER
4.25IN X 2.75IN

TITLE:
AUTHOR:
GENRE:
METHOD:
DATE STARTED:
DATE FINISHED:
WOULD YOU RECOMMEND?
NOTES & QUOTES:

BOOK COVER
4.25IN X 2.75IN

TITLE:
AUTHOR:
GENRE:
METHOD:
DATE STARTED:
DATE FINISHED:
WOULD YOU RECOMMEND?
NOTES & QUOTES:

BOOK COVER
4.25IN X 2.75IN

TITLE:

AUTHOR:

GENRE:

METHOD:

DATE STARTED:

DATE FINISHED:

WOULD YOU RECOMMEND?

NOTES & QUOTES:

BOOK COVER
4.25IN X 2.75IN

TITLE:

AUTHOR:

GENRE:

METHOD:

DATE STARTED:

DATE FINISHED:

WOULD YOU RECOMMEND?

NOTES & QUOTES:

BOOK COVER
4.25IN X 2.75IN

TITLE:
AUTHOR:
GENRE:
METHOD:
DATE STARTED:
DATE FINISHED:
WOULD YOU RECOMMEND?
NOTES & QUOTES:

BOOK COVER
4.25IN X 2.75IN

TITLE:
AUTHOR:
GENRE:
METHOD:
DATE STARTED:
DATE FINISHED:
WOULD YOU RECOMMEND?
NOTES & QUOTES:

BOOK COVER
4.25IN X 2.75IN

TITLE:

AUTHOR:

GENRE:

METHOD:

DATE STARTED:

DATE FINISHED:

WOULD YOU RECOMMEND?

NOTES & QUOTES:

BOOK COVER
4.25IN X 2.75IN

TITLE:

AUTHOR:

GENRE:

METHOD:

DATE STARTED:

DATE FINISHED:

WOULD YOU RECOMMEND?

NOTES & QUOTES:

BOOK COVER
4.25IN X 2.75IN

TITLE: _____
AUTHOR: _____
GENRE: _____
METHOD: _____
DATE STARTED: _____
DATE FINISHED: _____
WOULD YOU RECOMMEND? _____
NOTES & QUOTES:

☆ ☆ ☆ ☆ ☆

BOOK COVER
4.25IN X 2.75IN

TITLE: _____
AUTHOR: _____
GENRE: _____
METHOD: _____
DATE STARTED: _____
DATE FINISHED: _____
WOULD YOU RECOMMEND? _____
NOTES & QUOTES:

☆ ☆ ☆ ☆ ☆

BOOK COVER
4.25IN X 2.75IN

TITLE:
AUTHOR:
GENRE:
METHOD:
DATE STARTED:
DATE FINISHED:
WOULD YOU RECOMMEND?
NOTES & QUOTES:

★★★★★

BOOK COVER
4.25IN X 2.75IN

TITLE:
AUTHOR:
GENRE:
METHOD:
DATE STARTED:
DATE FINISHED:
WOULD YOU RECOMMEND?
NOTES & QUOTES:

★★★★★

BOOK COVER
4.25IN X 2.75IN

TITLE:

AUTHOR:

GENRE:

METHOD:

DATE STARTED:

DATE FINISHED:

WOULD YOU RECOMMEND?

NOTES & QUOTES:

BOOK COVER
4.25IN X 2.75IN

TITLE:

AUTHOR:

GENRE:

METHOD:

DATE STARTED:

DATE FINISHED:

WOULD YOU RECOMMEND?

NOTES & QUOTES:

BOOK COVER
4.25IN X 2.75IN

TITLE:

AUTHOR:

GENRE:

METHOD:

DATE STARTED:

DATE FINISHED:

WOULD YOU RECOMMEND?

NOTES & QUOTES:

⭐⭐⭐⭐⭐

BOOK COVER
4.25IN X 2.75IN

TITLE:

AUTHOR:

GENRE:

METHOD:

DATE STARTED:

DATE FINISHED:

WOULD YOU RECOMMEND?

NOTES & QUOTES:

⭐⭐⭐⭐⭐

BOOK COVER
4.25IN X 2.75IN

TITLE:
AUTHOR:
GENRE:
METHOD:
DATE STARTED:
DATE FINISHED:
WOULD YOU RECOMMEND?
NOTES & QUOTES:

☆☆☆☆☆

BOOK COVER
4.25IN X 2.75IN

TITLE:
AUTHOR:
GENRE:
METHOD:
DATE STARTED:
DATE FINISHED:
WOULD YOU RECOMMEND?
NOTES & QUOTES:

☆☆☆☆☆

BOOK COVER
4.25IN X 2.75IN

TITLE:

AUTHOR:

GENRE:

METHOD:

DATE STARTED:

DATE FINISHED:

WOULD YOU RECOMMEND?

NOTES & QUOTES:

⭐⭐⭐⭐⭐

BOOK COVER
4.25IN X 2.75IN

TITLE:

AUTHOR:

GENRE:

METHOD:

DATE STARTED:

DATE FINISHED:

WOULD YOU RECOMMEND?

NOTES & QUOTES:

⭐⭐⭐⭐⭐

BOOK COVER
4.25IN X 2.75IN

TITLE:
AUTHOR:
GENRE:
METHOD:
DATE STARTED:
DATE FINISHED:
WOULD YOU RECOMMEND?
NOTES & QUOTES:

BOOK COVER
4.25IN X 2.75IN

TITLE:
AUTHOR:
GENRE:
METHOD:
DATE STARTED:
DATE FINISHED:
WOULD YOU RECOMMEND?
NOTES & QUOTES:

BOOK COVER
4.25IN X 2.75IN

TITLE:

AUTHOR:

GENRE:

METHOD:

DATE STARTED:

DATE FINISHED:

WOULD YOU RECOMMEND?

NOTES & QUOTES:

BOOK COVER
4.25IN X 2.75IN

TITLE:

AUTHOR:

GENRE:

METHOD:

DATE STARTED:

DATE FINISHED:

WOULD YOU RECOMMEND?

NOTES & QUOTES:

BOOK COVER
4.25IN X 2.75IN

TITLE:

AUTHOR:

GENRE:

METHOD:

DATE STARTED:

DATE FINISHED:

WOULD YOU RECOMMEND?

NOTES & QUOTES:

BOOK COVER
4.25IN X 2.75IN

TITLE:

AUTHOR:

GENRE:

METHOD:

DATE STARTED:

DATE FINISHED:

WOULD YOU RECOMMEND?

NOTES & QUOTES:

BOOK COVER
4.25IN X 2.75IN

TITLE:
AUTHOR:
GENRE:
METHOD:
DATE STARTED:
DATE FINISHED:
WOULD YOU RECOMMEND?
NOTES & QUOTES:

★★★★★

BOOK COVER
4.25IN X 2.75IN

TITLE:
AUTHOR:
GENRE:
METHOD:
DATE STARTED:
DATE FINISHED:
WOULD YOU RECOMMEND?
NOTES & QUOTES:

★★★★★

BOOK COVER
4.25IN X 2.75IN

TITLE:
AUTHOR:
GENRE:
METHOD:
DATE STARTED:
DATE FINISHED:
WOULD YOU RECOMMEND?
NOTES & QUOTES:

BOOK COVER
4.25IN X 2.75IN

TITLE:
AUTHOR:
GENRE:
METHOD:
DATE STARTED:
DATE FINISHED:
WOULD YOU RECOMMEND?
NOTES & QUOTES:

BOOK COVER
4.25IN X 2.75IN

TITLE:
AUTHOR:
GENRE:
METHOD:
DATE STARTED:
DATE FINISHED:
WOULD YOU RECOMMEND?
NOTES & QUOTES:

★★★★★

BOOK COVER
4.25IN X 2.75IN

TITLE:
AUTHOR:
GENRE:
METHOD:
DATE STARTED:
DATE FINISHED:
WOULD YOU RECOMMEND?
NOTES & QUOTES:

★★★★★

BOOK COVER
4.25IN X 2.75IN

TITLE:
AUTHOR:
GENRE:
METHOD:
DATE STARTED:
DATE FINISHED:
WOULD YOU RECOMMEND?
NOTES & QUOTES:

BOOK COVER
4.25IN X 2.75IN

TITLE:
AUTHOR:
GENRE:
METHOD:
DATE STARTED:
DATE FINISHED:
WOULD YOU RECOMMEND?
NOTES & QUOTES:

BOOK COVER
4.25IN X 2.75IN

TITLE:
AUTHOR:
GENRE:
METHOD:
DATE STARTED:
DATE FINISHED:
WOULD YOU RECOMMEND?
NOTES & QUOTES:

★ ★ ★ ★ ★

BOOK COVER
4.25IN X 2.75IN

TITLE:
AUTHOR:
GENRE:
METHOD:
DATE STARTED:
DATE FINISHED:
WOULD YOU RECOMMEND?
NOTES & QUOTES:

★ ★ ★ ★ ★

BOOK COVER
4.25IN X 2.75IN

TITLE:

AUTHOR:

GENRE:

METHOD:

DATE STARTED:

DATE FINISHED:

WOULD YOU RECOMMEND?

NOTES & QUOTES:

BOOK COVER
4.25IN X 2.75IN

TITLE:

AUTHOR:

GENRE:

METHOD:

DATE STARTED:

DATE FINISHED:

WOULD YOU RECOMMEND?

NOTES & QUOTES:

BOOK COVER
4.25IN X 2.75IN

TITLE:

AUTHOR:

GENRE:

METHOD:

DATE STARTED:

DATE FINISHED:

WOULD YOU RECOMMEND?

NOTES & QUOTES:

BOOK COVER
4.25IN X 2.75IN

TITLE:

AUTHOR:

GENRE:

METHOD:

DATE STARTED:

DATE FINISHED:

WOULD YOU RECOMMEND?

NOTES & QUOTES:

BOOK COVER
4.25IN X 2.75IN

TITLE:

AUTHOR:

GENRE:

METHOD:

DATE STARTED:

DATE FINISHED:

WOULD YOU RECOMMEND?

NOTES & QUOTES:

BOOK COVER
4.25IN X 2.75IN

TITLE:

AUTHOR:

GENRE:

METHOD:

DATE STARTED:

DATE FINISHED:

WOULD YOU RECOMMEND?

NOTES & QUOTES:

BOOK COVER
4.25IN X 2.75IN

TITLE:
AUTHOR:
GENRE:
METHOD:
DATE STARTED:
DATE FINISHED:
WOULD YOU RECOMMEND?
NOTES & QUOTES:

★ ★ ★ ★ ★

BOOK COVER
4.25IN X 2.75IN

TITLE:
AUTHOR:
GENRE:
METHOD:
DATE STARTED:
DATE FINISHED:
WOULD YOU RECOMMEND?
NOTES & QUOTES:

★ ★ ★ ★ ★

BOOK COVER
4.25IN X 2.75IN

TITLE: _____
AUTHOR: _____
GENRE: _____
METHOD: _____
DATE STARTED: _____
DATE FINISHED: _____
WOULD YOU RECOMMEND? _____
NOTES & QUOTES:

★ ★ ★ ★ ★

BOOK COVER
4.25IN X 2.75IN

TITLE: _____
AUTHOR: _____
GENRE: _____
METHOD: _____
DATE STARTED: _____
DATE FINISHED: _____
WOULD YOU RECOMMEND? _____
NOTES & QUOTES:

★ ★ ★ ★ ★

BOOK COVER
4.25IN X 2.75IN

TITLE:

AUTHOR:

GENRE:

METHOD:

DATE STARTED:

DATE FINISHED:

WOULD YOU RECOMMEND?

NOTES & QUOTES:

★★★★★

BOOK COVER
4.25IN X 2.75IN

TITLE:

AUTHOR:

GENRE:

METHOD:

DATE STARTED:

DATE FINISHED:

WOULD YOU RECOMMEND?

NOTES & QUOTES:

★★★★★

BOOK COVER
4.25IN X 2.75IN

TITLE:
AUTHOR:
GENRE:
METHOD:
DATE STARTED:
DATE FINISHED:
WOULD YOU RECOMMEND?
NOTES & QUOTES:

BOOK COVER
4.25IN X 2.75IN

TITLE:
AUTHOR:
GENRE:
METHOD:
DATE STARTED:
DATE FINISHED:
WOULD YOU RECOMMEND?
NOTES & QUOTES:

BOOK COVER
4.25IN X 2.75IN

TITLE:

AUTHOR:

GENRE:

METHOD:

DATE STARTED:

DATE FINISHED:

WOULD YOU RECOMMEND?

NOTES & QUOTES:

★★★★★

BOOK COVER
4.25IN X 2.75IN

TITLE:

AUTHOR:

GENRE:

METHOD:

DATE STARTED:

DATE FINISHED:

WOULD YOU RECOMMEND?

NOTES & QUOTES:

★★★★★

BOOK COVER
4.25IN X 2.75IN

TITLE:
AUTHOR:
GENRE:
METHOD:
DATE STARTED:
DATE FINISHED:
WOULD YOU RECOMMEND?
NOTES & QUOTES:

⭐ ⭐ ⭐ ⭐ ⭐

BOOK COVER
4.25IN X 2.75IN

TITLE:
AUTHOR:
GENRE:
METHOD:
DATE STARTED:
DATE FINISHED:
WOULD YOU RECOMMEND?
NOTES & QUOTES:

⭐ ⭐ ⭐ ⭐ ⭐

BOOK COVER
4.25IN X 2.75IN

TITLE:

AUTHOR:

GENRE:

METHOD:

DATE STARTED:

DATE FINISHED:

WOULD YOU RECOMMEND?

NOTES & QUOTES:

★★★★★

BOOK COVER
4.25IN X 2.75IN

TITLE:

AUTHOR:

GENRE:

METHOD:

DATE STARTED:

DATE FINISHED:

WOULD YOU RECOMMEND?

NOTES & QUOTES:

★★★★★

BOOK COVER
4.25IN X 2.75IN

TITLE:

AUTHOR:

GENRE:

METHOD:

DATE STARTED:

DATE FINISHED:

WOULD YOU RECOMMEND?

NOTES & QUOTES:

☆☆☆☆☆

BOOK COVER
4.25IN X 2.75IN

TITLE:

AUTHOR:

GENRE:

METHOD:

DATE STARTED:

DATE FINISHED:

WOULD YOU RECOMMEND?

NOTES & QUOTES:

☆☆☆☆☆

BOOK COVER
4.25IN X 2.75IN

TITLE:
AUTHOR:
GENRE:
METHOD:
DATE STARTED:
DATE FINISHED:
WOULD YOU RECOMMEND?
NOTES & QUOTES:

★ ★ ★ ★ ★

BOOK COVER
4.25IN X 2.75IN

TITLE:
AUTHOR:
GENRE:
METHOD:
DATE STARTED:
DATE FINISHED:
WOULD YOU RECOMMEND?
NOTES & QUOTES:

★ ★ ★ ★ ★

BOOK COVER
4.25IN X 2.75IN

TITLE:
AUTHOR:
GENRE:
METHOD:
DATE STARTED:
DATE FINISHED:
WOULD YOU RECOMMEND?
NOTES & QUOTES:

BOOK COVER
4.25IN X 2.75IN

TITLE:
AUTHOR:
GENRE:
METHOD:
DATE STARTED:
DATE FINISHED:
WOULD YOU RECOMMEND?
NOTES & QUOTES:

BOOK COVER
4.25IN X 2.75IN

★★★★★

TITLE: _____
AUTHOR: _____
GENRE: _____
METHOD: _____
DATE STARTED: _____
DATE FINISHED: _____
WOULD YOU RECOMMEND? _____
NOTES & QUOTES:

BOOK COVER
4.25IN X 2.75IN

★★★★★

TITLE: _____
AUTHOR: _____
GENRE: _____
METHOD: _____
DATE STARTED: _____
DATE FINISHED: _____
WOULD YOU RECOMMEND? _____
NOTES & QUOTES:

BOOK COVER
4.25IN X 2.75IN

TITLE:

AUTHOR:

GENRE:

METHOD:

DATE STARTED:

DATE FINISHED:

WOULD YOU RECOMMEND?

NOTES & QUOTES:

BOOK COVER
4.25IN X 2.75IN

TITLE:

AUTHOR:

GENRE:

METHOD:

DATE STARTED:

DATE FINISHED:

WOULD YOU RECOMMEND?

NOTES & QUOTES:

BOOK COVER
4.25IN X 2.75IN

TITLE:
AUTHOR:
GENRE:
METHOD:
DATE STARTED:
DATE FINISHED:
WOULD YOU RECOMMEND?
NOTES & QUOTES:

BOOK COVER
4.25IN X 2.75IN

TITLE:
AUTHOR:
GENRE:
METHOD:
DATE STARTED:
DATE FINISHED:
WOULD YOU RECOMMEND?
NOTES & QUOTES:

BOOK COVER
4.25IN X 2.75IN

TITLE:

AUTHOR:

GENRE:

METHOD:

DATE STARTED:

DATE FINISHED:

WOULD YOU RECOMMEND?

NOTES & QUOTES:

BOOK COVER
4.25IN X 2.75IN

TITLE:

AUTHOR:

GENRE:

METHOD:

DATE STARTED:

DATE FINISHED:

WOULD YOU RECOMMEND?

NOTES & QUOTES:

BOOK COVER
4.25IN X 2.75IN

TITLE:
AUTHOR:
GENRE:
METHOD:
DATE STARTED:
DATE FINISHED:
WOULD YOU RECOMMEND?
NOTES & QUOTES:

BOOK COVER
4.25IN X 2.75IN

TITLE:
AUTHOR:
GENRE:
METHOD:
DATE STARTED:
DATE FINISHED:
WOULD YOU RECOMMEND?
NOTES & QUOTES:

BOOK COVER
4.25IN X 2.75IN

TITLE:

AUTHOR:

GENRE:

METHOD:

DATE STARTED:

DATE FINISHED:

WOULD YOU RECOMMEND?

NOTES & QUOTES:

BOOK COVER
4.25IN X 2.75IN

TITLE:

AUTHOR:

GENRE:

METHOD:

DATE STARTED:

DATE FINISHED:

WOULD YOU RECOMMEND?

NOTES & QUOTES:

BOOK COVER
4.25IN X 2.75IN

TITLE:
AUTHOR:
GENRE:
METHOD:
DATE STARTED:
DATE FINISHED:
WOULD YOU RECOMMEND?
NOTES & QUOTES:

BOOK COVER
4.25IN X 2.75IN

TITLE:
AUTHOR:
GENRE:
METHOD:
DATE STARTED:
DATE FINISHED:
WOULD YOU RECOMMEND?
NOTES & QUOTES:

BOOK COVER
4.25IN X 2.75IN

TITLE:
AUTHOR:
GENRE:
METHOD:
DATE STARTED:
DATE FINISHED:
WOULD YOU RECOMMEND?
NOTES & QUOTES:

BOOK COVER
4.25IN X 2.75IN

TITLE:
AUTHOR:
GENRE:
METHOD:
DATE STARTED:
DATE FINISHED:
WOULD YOU RECOMMEND?
NOTES & QUOTES:

BOOK COVER
4.25IN X 2.75IN

TITLE:

AUTHOR:

GENRE:

METHOD:

DATE STARTED:

DATE FINISHED:

WOULD YOU RECOMMEND?

NOTES & QUOTES:

★★★★★

BOOK COVER
4.25IN X 2.75IN

TITLE:

AUTHOR:

GENRE:

METHOD:

DATE STARTED:

DATE FINISHED:

WOULD YOU RECOMMEND?

NOTES & QUOTES:

★★★★★

BOOK COVER
4.25IN X 2.75IN

TITLE:
AUTHOR:
GENRE:
METHOD:
DATE STARTED:
DATE FINISHED:
WOULD YOU RECOMMEND?
NOTES & QUOTES:

BOOK COVER
4.25IN X 2.75IN

TITLE:
AUTHOR:
GENRE:
METHOD:
DATE STARTED:
DATE FINISHED:
WOULD YOU RECOMMEND?
NOTES & QUOTES:

BOOK COVER
4.25IN X 2.75IN

TITLE:

AUTHOR:

GENRE:

METHOD:

DATE STARTED:

DATE FINISHED:

WOULD YOU RECOMMEND?

NOTES & QUOTES:

⭐ ⭐ ⭐ ⭐ ⭐

BOOK COVER
4.25IN X 2.75IN

TITLE:

AUTHOR:

GENRE:

METHOD:

DATE STARTED:

DATE FINISHED:

WOULD YOU RECOMMEND?

NOTES & QUOTES:

⭐ ⭐ ⭐ ⭐ ⭐

BOOK COVER
4.25IN X 2.75IN

TITLE:
AUTHOR:
GENRE:
METHOD:
DATE STARTED:
DATE FINISHED:
WOULD YOU RECOMMEND?
NOTES & QUOTES:

★★★★★

BOOK COVER
4.25IN X 2.75IN

TITLE:
AUTHOR:
GENRE:
METHOD:
DATE STARTED:
DATE FINISHED:
WOULD YOU RECOMMEND?
NOTES & QUOTES:

★★★★★

BOOK COVER
4.25IN X 2.75IN

TITLE:
AUTHOR:
GENRE:
METHOD:
DATE STARTED:
DATE FINISHED:
WOULD YOU RECOMMEND?
NOTES & QUOTES:

BOOK COVER
4.25IN X 2.75IN

TITLE:
AUTHOR:
GENRE:
METHOD:
DATE STARTED:
DATE FINISHED:
WOULD YOU RECOMMEND?
NOTES & QUOTES:

BOOK COVER
4.25IN X 2.75IN

TITLE:

AUTHOR:

GENRE:

METHOD:

DATE STARTED:

DATE FINISHED:

WOULD YOU RECOMMEND?

NOTES & QUOTES:

BOOK COVER
4.25IN X 2.75IN

TITLE:

AUTHOR:

GENRE:

METHOD:

DATE STARTED:

DATE FINISHED:

WOULD YOU RECOMMEND?

NOTES & QUOTES:

BOOK COVER
4.25IN X 2.75IN

TITLE:

AUTHOR:

GENRE:

METHOD:

DATE STARTED:

DATE FINISHED:

WOULD YOU RECOMMEND?

NOTES & QUOTES:

★★★★★

BOOK COVER
4.25IN X 2.75IN

TITLE:

AUTHOR:

GENRE:

METHOD:

DATE STARTED:

DATE FINISHED:

WOULD YOU RECOMMEND?

NOTES & QUOTES:

★★★★★

BOOK COVER
4.25IN X 2.75IN

TITLE:
AUTHOR:
GENRE:
METHOD:
DATE STARTED:
DATE FINISHED:
WOULD YOU RECOMMEND?
NOTES & QUOTES:

BOOK COVER
4.25IN X 2.75IN

TITLE:
AUTHOR:
GENRE:
METHOD:
DATE STARTED:
DATE FINISHED:
WOULD YOU RECOMMEND?
NOTES & QUOTES:

BOOK COVER
4.25IN X 2.75IN

TITLE:
AUTHOR:
GENRE:
METHOD:
DATE STARTED:
DATE FINISHED:
WOULD YOU RECOMMEND?
NOTES & QUOTES:

⭐⭐⭐⭐⭐

BOOK COVER
4.25IN X 2.75IN

TITLE:
AUTHOR:
GENRE:
METHOD:
DATE STARTED:
DATE FINISHED:
WOULD YOU RECOMMEND?
NOTES & QUOTES:

⭐⭐⭐⭐⭐

BOOK COVER
4.25IN X 2.75IN

TITLE:

AUTHOR:

GENRE:

METHOD:

DATE STARTED:

DATE FINISHED:

WOULD YOU RECOMMEND?

NOTES & QUOTES:

BOOK COVER
4.25IN X 2.75IN

TITLE:

AUTHOR:

GENRE:

METHOD:

DATE STARTED:

DATE FINISHED:

WOULD YOU RECOMMEND?

NOTES & QUOTES:

BOOK COVER
4.25IN X 2.75IN

TITLE:
AUTHOR:
GENRE:
METHOD:
DATE STARTED:
DATE FINISHED:
WOULD YOU RECOMMEND?
NOTES & QUOTES:

BOOK COVER
4.25IN X 2.75IN

TITLE:
AUTHOR:
GENRE:
METHOD:
DATE STARTED:
DATE FINISHED:
WOULD YOU RECOMMEND?
NOTES & QUOTES:

BOOK COVER
4.25IN X 2.75IN

TITLE:
AUTHOR:
GENRE:
METHOD:
DATE STARTED:
DATE FINISHED:
WOULD YOU RECOMMEND?
NOTES & QUOTES:

BOOK COVER
4.25IN X 2.75IN

TITLE:
AUTHOR:
GENRE:
METHOD:
DATE STARTED:
DATE FINISHED:
WOULD YOU RECOMMEND?
NOTES & QUOTES:

BOOK COVER
4.25IN X 2.75IN

TITLE:

AUTHOR:

GENRE:

METHOD:

DATE STARTED:

DATE FINISHED:

WOULD YOU RECOMMEND?

NOTES & QUOTES:

★★★★★

BOOK COVER
4.25IN X 2.75IN

TITLE:

AUTHOR:

GENRE:

METHOD:

DATE STARTED:

DATE FINISHED:

WOULD YOU RECOMMEND?

NOTES & QUOTES:

★★★★★

BOOK COVER
4.25IN X 2.75IN

TITLE:
AUTHOR:
GENRE:
METHOD:
DATE STARTED:
DATE FINISHED:
WOULD YOU RECOMMEND?
NOTES & QUOTES:

BOOK COVER
4.25IN X 2.75IN

TITLE:
AUTHOR:
GENRE:
METHOD:
DATE STARTED:
DATE FINISHED:
WOULD YOU RECOMMEND?
NOTES & QUOTES:

BOOK COVER
4.25IN X 2.75IN

TITLE:
AUTHOR:
GENRE:
METHOD:
DATE STARTED:
DATE FINISHED:
WOULD YOU RECOMMEND?
NOTES & QUOTES:

★★★★★

BOOK COVER
4.25IN X 2.75IN

TITLE:
AUTHOR:
GENRE:
METHOD:
DATE STARTED:
DATE FINISHED:
WOULD YOU RECOMMEND?
NOTES & QUOTES:

★★★★★

BOOK COVER
4.25IN X 2.75IN

TITLE:
AUTHOR:
GENRE:
METHOD:
DATE STARTED:
DATE FINISHED:
WOULD YOU RECOMMEND?
NOTES & QUOTES:

BOOK COVER
4.25IN X 2.75IN

TITLE:
AUTHOR:
GENRE:
METHOD:
DATE STARTED:
DATE FINISHED:
WOULD YOU RECOMMEND?
NOTES & QUOTES:

BOOK COVER
4.25IN X 2.75IN

TITLE:

AUTHOR:

GENRE:

METHOD:

DATE STARTED:

DATE FINISHED:

WOULD YOU RECOMMEND?

NOTES & QUOTES:

★★★★★

BOOK COVER
4.25IN X 2.75IN

TITLE:

AUTHOR:

GENRE:

METHOD:

DATE STARTED:

DATE FINISHED:

WOULD YOU RECOMMEND?

NOTES & QUOTES:

★★★★★

BOOK COVER
4.25IN X 2.75IN

TITLE:
AUTHOR:
GENRE:
METHOD:
DATE STARTED:
DATE FINISHED:
WOULD YOU RECOMMEND?
NOTES & QUOTES:

BOOK COVER
4.25IN X 2.75IN

TITLE:
AUTHOR:
GENRE:
METHOD:
DATE STARTED:
DATE FINISHED:
WOULD YOU RECOMMEND?
NOTES & QUOTES:

BOOK COVER
4.25IN X 2.75IN

TITLE:
AUTHOR:
GENRE:
METHOD:
DATE STARTED:
DATE FINISHED:
WOULD YOU RECOMMEND?
NOTES & QUOTES:

BOOK COVER
4.25IN X 2.75IN

TITLE:
AUTHOR:
GENRE:
METHOD:
DATE STARTED:
DATE FINISHED:
WOULD YOU RECOMMEND?
NOTES & QUOTES:

BOOK COVER
4.25IN X 2.75IN

TITLE:
AUTHOR:
GENRE:
METHOD:
DATE STARTED:
DATE FINISHED:
WOULD YOU RECOMMEND?
NOTES & QUOTES:

BOOK COVER
4.25IN X 2.75IN

TITLE:
AUTHOR:
GENRE:
METHOD:
DATE STARTED:
DATE FINISHED:
WOULD YOU RECOMMEND?
NOTES & QUOTES:

BOOK COVER
4.25IN X 2.75IN

TITLE:
AUTHOR:
GENRE:
METHOD:
DATE STARTED:
DATE FINISHED:
WOULD YOU RECOMMEND?
NOTES & QUOTES:

BOOK COVER
4.25IN X 2.75IN

TITLE:
AUTHOR:
GENRE:
METHOD:
DATE STARTED:
DATE FINISHED:
WOULD YOU RECOMMEND?
NOTES & QUOTES:

BOOK COVER
4.25IN X 2.75IN

TITLE:
AUTHOR:
GENRE:
METHOD:
DATE STARTED:
DATE FINISHED:
WOULD YOU RECOMMEND?
NOTES & QUOTES:

BOOK COVER
4.25IN X 2.75IN

TITLE:
AUTHOR:
GENRE:
METHOD:
DATE STARTED:
DATE FINISHED:
WOULD YOU RECOMMEND?
NOTES & QUOTES:

BOOK COVER
4.25IN X 2.75IN

TITLE:

AUTHOR:

GENRE:

METHOD:

DATE STARTED:

DATE FINISHED:

WOULD YOU RECOMMEND?

NOTES & QUOTES:

★★★★★

BOOK COVER
4.25IN X 2.75IN

TITLE:

AUTHOR:

GENRE:

METHOD:

DATE STARTED:

DATE FINISHED:

WOULD YOU RECOMMEND?

NOTES & QUOTES:

★★★★★

BOOK COVER
4.25IN X 2.75IN

TITLE: _____
AUTHOR: _____
GENRE: _____
METHOD: _____
DATE STARTED: _____
DATE FINISHED: _____
WOULD YOU RECOMMEND? _____
NOTES & QUOTES:

★★★★★

BOOK COVER
4.25IN X 2.75IN

TITLE: _____
AUTHOR: _____
GENRE: _____
METHOD: _____
DATE STARTED: _____
DATE FINISHED: _____
WOULD YOU RECOMMEND? _____
NOTES & QUOTES:

★★★★★

BOOK COVER
4.25IN X 2.75IN

TITLE:
AUTHOR:
GENRE:
METHOD:
DATE STARTED:
DATE FINISHED:
WOULD YOU RECOMMEND?
NOTES & QUOTES:

BOOK COVER
4.25IN X 2.75IN

TITLE:
AUTHOR:
GENRE:
METHOD:
DATE STARTED:
DATE FINISHED:
WOULD YOU RECOMMEND?
NOTES & QUOTES:

BOOK COVER
4.25IN X 2.75IN

TITLE:
AUTHOR:
GENRE:
METHOD:
DATE STARTED:
DATE FINISHED:
WOULD YOU RECOMMEND?
NOTES & QUOTES:

BOOK COVER
4.25IN X 2.75IN

TITLE:
AUTHOR:
GENRE:
METHOD:
DATE STARTED:
DATE FINISHED:
WOULD YOU RECOMMEND?
NOTES & QUOTES:

BOOK COVER
4.25IN X 2.75IN

TITLE:

AUTHOR:

GENRE:

METHOD:

DATE STARTED:

DATE FINISHED:

WOULD YOU RECOMMEND?

NOTES & QUOTES:

★★★★★

BOOK COVER
4.25IN X 2.75IN

TITLE:

AUTHOR:

GENRE:

METHOD:

DATE STARTED:

DATE FINISHED:

WOULD YOU RECOMMEND?

NOTES & QUOTES:

★★★★★

BOOK COVER
4.25IN X 2.75IN

TITLE:
AUTHOR:
GENRE:
METHOD:
DATE STARTED:
DATE FINISHED:
WOULD YOU RECOMMEND?
NOTES & QUOTES:

BOOK COVER
4.25IN X 2.75IN

TITLE:
AUTHOR:
GENRE:
METHOD:
DATE STARTED:
DATE FINISHED:
WOULD YOU RECOMMEND?
NOTES & QUOTES:

BOOK COVER
4.25IN X 2.75IN

TITLE:
AUTHOR:
GENRE:
METHOD:
DATE STARTED:
DATE FINISHED:
WOULD YOU RECOMMEND?
NOTES & QUOTES:

BOOK COVER
4.25IN X 2.75IN

TITLE:
AUTHOR:
GENRE:
METHOD:
DATE STARTED:
DATE FINISHED:
WOULD YOU RECOMMEND?
NOTES & QUOTES:

BOOK COVER
4.25IN X 2.75IN

TITLE:
AUTHOR:
GENRE:
METHOD:
DATE STARTED:
DATE FINISHED:
WOULD YOU RECOMMEND?
NOTES & QUOTES:

★★★★★

BOOK COVER
4.25IN X 2.75IN

TITLE:
AUTHOR:
GENRE:
METHOD:
DATE STARTED:
DATE FINISHED:
WOULD YOU RECOMMEND?
NOTES & QUOTES:

★★★★★

BOOK COVER
4.25IN X 2.75IN

TITLE:
AUTHOR:
GENRE:
METHOD:
DATE STARTED:
DATE FINISHED:
WOULD YOU RECOMMEND?
NOTES & QUOTES:

★★★★★

BOOK COVER
4.25IN X 2.75IN

TITLE:
AUTHOR:
GENRE:
METHOD:
DATE STARTED:
DATE FINISHED:
WOULD YOU RECOMMEND?
NOTES & QUOTES:

★★★★★

BOOK COVER
4.25IN X 2.75IN

TITLE:
AUTHOR:
GENRE:
METHOD:
DATE STARTED:
DATE FINISHED:
WOULD YOU RECOMMEND?
NOTES & QUOTES:

BOOK COVER
4.25IN X 2.75IN

TITLE:
AUTHOR:
GENRE:
METHOD:
DATE STARTED:
DATE FINISHED:
WOULD YOU RECOMMEND?
NOTES & QUOTES:

BOOK COVER
4.25IN X 2.75IN

TITLE:
AUTHOR:
GENRE:
METHOD:
DATE STARTED:
DATE FINISHED:
WOULD YOU RECOMMEND?
NOTES & QUOTES:

BOOK COVER
4.25IN X 2.75IN

TITLE:
AUTHOR:
GENRE:
METHOD:
DATE STARTED:
DATE FINISHED:
WOULD YOU RECOMMEND?
NOTES & QUOTES:

BOOK COVER
4.25IN X 2.75IN

TITLE:

AUTHOR:

GENRE:

METHOD:

DATE STARTED:

DATE FINISHED:

WOULD YOU RECOMMEND?

NOTES & QUOTES:

BOOK COVER
4.25IN X 2.75IN

TITLE:

AUTHOR:

GENRE:

METHOD:

DATE STARTED:

DATE FINISHED:

WOULD YOU RECOMMEND?

NOTES & QUOTES:

BOOK COVER
4.25IN X 2.75IN

TITLE:
AUTHOR:
GENRE:
METHOD:
DATE STARTED:
DATE FINISHED:
WOULD YOU RECOMMEND?
NOTES & QUOTES:

BOOK COVER
4.25IN X 2.75IN

TITLE:
AUTHOR:
GENRE:
METHOD:
DATE STARTED:
DATE FINISHED:
WOULD YOU RECOMMEND?
NOTES & QUOTES:

BOOK COVER
4.25IN X 2.75IN

TITLE:
AUTHOR:
GENRE:
METHOD:
DATE STARTED:
DATE FINISHED:
WOULD YOU RECOMMEND?
NOTES & QUOTES:

BOOK COVER
4.25IN X 2.75IN

TITLE:
AUTHOR:
GENRE:
METHOD:
DATE STARTED:
DATE FINISHED:
WOULD YOU RECOMMEND?
NOTES & QUOTES:

BOOK COVER
4.25IN X 2.75IN

TITLE:

AUTHOR:

GENRE:

METHOD:

DATE STARTED:

DATE FINISHED:

WOULD YOU RECOMMEND?

NOTES & QUOTES:

BOOK COVER
4.25IN X 2.75IN

TITLE:

AUTHOR:

GENRE:

METHOD:

DATE STARTED:

DATE FINISHED:

WOULD YOU RECOMMEND?

NOTES & QUOTES:

BOOK COVER
4.25IN X 2.75IN

TITLE:
AUTHOR:
GENRE:
METHOD:
DATE STARTED:
DATE FINISHED:
WOULD YOU RECOMMEND?
NOTES & QUOTES:

⭐⭐⭐⭐⭐

BOOK COVER
4.25IN X 2.75IN

TITLE:
AUTHOR:
GENRE:
METHOD:
DATE STARTED:
DATE FINISHED:
WOULD YOU RECOMMEND?
NOTES & QUOTES:

⭐⭐⭐⭐⭐

BOOK COVER
4.25IN X 2.75IN

TITLE:
AUTHOR:
GENRE:
METHOD:
DATE STARTED:
DATE FINISHED:
WOULD YOU RECOMMEND?
NOTES & QUOTES:

BOOK COVER
4.25IN X 2.75IN

TITLE:
AUTHOR:
GENRE:
METHOD:
DATE STARTED:
DATE FINISHED:
WOULD YOU RECOMMEND?
NOTES & QUOTES:

BOOK COVER
4.25IN X 2.75IN

TITLE:
AUTHOR:
GENRE:
METHOD:
DATE STARTED:
DATE FINISHED:
WOULD YOU RECOMMEND?
NOTES & QUOTES:

BOOK COVER
4.25IN X 2.75IN

TITLE:
AUTHOR:
GENRE:
METHOD:
DATE STARTED:
DATE FINISHED:
WOULD YOU RECOMMEND?
NOTES & QUOTES:

BOOK COVER
4.25IN X 2.75IN

TITLE:

AUTHOR:

GENRE:

METHOD:

DATE STARTED:

DATE FINISHED:

WOULD YOU RECOMMEND?

NOTES & QUOTES:

⭐⭐⭐⭐⭐

BOOK COVER
4.25IN X 2.75IN

TITLE:

AUTHOR:

GENRE:

METHOD:

DATE STARTED:

DATE FINISHED:

WOULD YOU RECOMMEND?

NOTES & QUOTES:

⭐⭐⭐⭐⭐

BOOK COVER
4.25IN X 2.75IN

TITLE: _____
AUTHOR: _____
GENRE: _____
METHOD: _____
DATE STARTED: _____
DATE FINISHED: _____
WOULD YOU RECOMMEND? _____
NOTES & QUOTES:

☆ ☆ ☆ ☆ ☆

BOOK COVER
4.25IN X 2.75IN

TITLE: _____
AUTHOR: _____
GENRE: _____
METHOD: _____
DATE STARTED: _____
DATE FINISHED: _____
WOULD YOU RECOMMEND? _____
NOTES & QUOTES:

☆ ☆ ☆ ☆ ☆

BOOK COVER
4.25IN X 2.75IN

TITLE:

AUTHOR:

GENRE:

METHOD:

DATE STARTED:

DATE FINISHED:

WOULD YOU RECOMMEND?

NOTES & QUOTES:

BOOK COVER
4.25IN X 2.75IN

TITLE:

AUTHOR:

GENRE:

METHOD:

DATE STARTED:

DATE FINISHED:

WOULD YOU RECOMMEND?

NOTES & QUOTES:

BOOK COVER
4.25IN X 2.75IN

TITLE:
AUTHOR:
GENRE:
METHOD:
DATE STARTED:
DATE FINISHED:
WOULD YOU RECOMMEND?
NOTES & QUOTES:

BOOK COVER
4.25IN X 2.75IN

TITLE:
AUTHOR:
GENRE:
METHOD:
DATE STARTED:
DATE FINISHED:
WOULD YOU RECOMMEND?
NOTES & QUOTES:

BOOK COVER
4.25IN X 2.75IN

TITLE:
AUTHOR:
GENRE:
METHOD:
DATE STARTED:
DATE FINISHED:
WOULD YOU RECOMMEND?
NOTES & QUOTES:

★★★★★

BOOK COVER
4.25IN X 2.75IN

TITLE:
AUTHOR:
GENRE:
METHOD:
DATE STARTED:
DATE FINISHED:
WOULD YOU RECOMMEND?
NOTES & QUOTES:

★★★★★

TO BE READ...

TO BE READ...

TO BE READ...

TO BE READ...

TO BE READ...

TO BE READ...

TO BE READ... ## TO BE READ...

TO BE READ...

TO BE READ...

Printed in Poland
by Amazon Fulfillment
Poland Sp. z o.o., Wrocław
03 June 2023

ee69ced2-a3a3-4a9f-9b19-c1f55de7f6e8R01